Enneagram

Modern Day Enneagram Discovery Of Yourself And Others Through Personality Types And Subtypes Guiding You Towards Purpose, Awareness, Self Knowledge And Healthy Relationships

Alex Fletcher

Table of Contents

Introduction: A Guide to Spiritual Transformation

The enneagram is a powerful type of gateway towards the understanding of others and self-awareness. It gives a description of different dynamics and structures concerning the major personality types by creating a path to a life which is more integrated and rewarding. It comes from the Greek word 'ennea' which loosely translates to nine, and 'grammos' that entails a written symbol.

So these are nine distinct strategies for relating to the self and others. Each type for the enneagram represents a different thought approach that comes from a different inner motivation and perspective of the world. The enneagram enables a better understanding thus through universal language which transcends nationality, culture, religion and even gender.

Your enneagram core functions as a home base from which one can make sense of integration and individuation. It is crucial to keep in mind that different enneagrams can display similar behavior. The styles are not based solely according to behavior and outward representations can be deceiving.

In order to distinguish between the different enneagrams, one has to access motivation in order to explore the reasons why people may choose to act in a particular manner and why acting in this way is given value by that person.

History of the enneagram

The earliest references for the enneagram as historically documented would be in the sacred geometry of the Pythagoreans that were interested in the deeper meaning of numbers 4000 years ago. This is a line of mystical mathematics which then went to Plato and Plotinus. There are some that believe the tradition was then assimilated into esoteric Judaism through a Jewish Neo Platonist philosopher where it is represented as the tree of life in the symbolism that relates to the nine folds. There are other variations of the symbol that can be seen in Islamic Sufi traditions also.

During the 1300s, the Naqshbandi order of Sufism which was the 'brotherhood of the bees', allegedly preserved and passed on the enneagram traditions. After that, it is said that it found its way into esoteric Christianity through Pseudo Dionysius and via Ramon Lull. More concrete understanding concerning the enneagram in recent history is from George Gurdjieff, a Russian teacher of esoteric knowledge who was a contemporary of Freud. Gurdjieff considered the enneagram as having the key to all knowledge which lay in the universe. He used the enneagram to explain the laws concerning creation and implies how he got to know about the enneagram in the 20s during his visit to the Sufi Sarmouni monastery, in Afghanistan.

In another part of the world, the enneagram teachings sprung up through Oscar Ichazo as part of the Africa Training in South America. The enneagram was apparently found to organize the different laws operating in the human person. While Gurdjieff used the process of the enneagram for all reality including the human individual, Ichazo made better use of the figure and dynamics for explaining the functioning of the human psyche. Another psychologist, Claudio Naranjo took up from where Ichazo left off and brought the enneagram further into western psychology during the 90s by framing the concepts into contemporary psychological language.

An evaluation concerning the origins of the enneagram and its teachings is defined in terms of the characteristic limitations of particular personality modes. The issue from that redefinition derives from the part that according to the enneagram teaching every individual has to choose a personality type as the basic strategy for coping with the environment that you may be in at the moment. All personality types happen to have their intrinsic motivations as sinning

2

becomes inevitable apparent. If sin is inevitable as it is resultant from one personality type, that would mean the solution to sin is found in the compensation of ones personality through following the prescriptions given by the enneagram. The remedy of sinning becomes a matter of great knowledge as opposed to reformation of the will. In Christianity, the sin is an unhealthy behavior and can be countered through improved understanding as it is a moral problem at the roots before God. The teachings given by the enneagram obscures the Christian understanding when it comes to sin because the origins are pagan.

There are a number of theoretical papers which have tried to develop potential applications for the enneagram. In business, the enneagram has been integrated into a theoretical paper that presents new frameworks for the acquisition of knowledge which proposes that the enneagram be utilized in order to develop and integrate knowledge within the social sciences. There was a paper on market segmentation that came up with the suggestion of utilizing enneagram typology in order to initiate marketing strategies for the market segments in the region done by Kamieni in 2005. The suggestions for improving spirituality in the work environment recommended the introduction of the enneagram as means for the corporations to create a company which was more harmonious and profitable.

Why it's true

The enneagram tradition defines personality as the lifetime accumulation for the emotional and mental patterns that constitute the persona. This being the individual that believes themselves to be and the way they are presented to the world.

These patterns may include the habitual ways of thought, perceptions and feelings. The words such as ego, personality and false sense of self are similar and used very interchangeably with the teachings that are propagated through the enneagram. The personality is claimed to be an imitation of the true self. It is fixated and reacts to the outer environment which is changing all the time with predictable and conditioned reactions. That being said, it is possible to claim the personality that we have gotten used to, as opposed to who we really are. The real being or the true self could be considered as a process rather than the fixed identity. Essence flows are changeable and they respond fresh and appropriately considering the altering situations of the outer environment.

Determination of an individual's personality type with the use of the enneagram system does not necessarily put one inside a defined box of nine archetypes. It assists people to see the box from where they are able to experience the world. With this in mind, one can step outside their worldview. Ideally speaking, personality is effective in allowing one to express themselves because they are able to categorize and identify who they really are. At the same time there can be issues when people get stuck in automatic habits. In discovering these unconscious patterns, people are able to lead lives which are more fulfilling and enjoy relationships which are overall healthier. Working within the enneagram model allows people to become successful in their relationships at home and within the working environment. Through understanding automatic reactions and blind spots, people can become more flexible with others in their lives and understand what others are feeling and thinking. This making it easier to tolerate other and be more compassionate. It also helps people to not take the negative reactions or their hostility in such a manner that it is personal. Through the identification of how you are emotionally and psychologically defensive, the enneagram allow you to have a chance at profound growth. At another level it also allows you to develop your relationship with yourself and better this, so that you can become more productive towards yourself and anything within your life.

Simply, the enneagram enables and grows ones capacity when it comes to self-observation. It provides vision for how the healthiest manifestation of people's types can look. Using this detail, it sets a path for the manner in getting to a higher level of awareness. Each type within the enneagram has particular behaviors that satisfy its needs and desires. This is the main strategy of the particular type in life. That would be driving much of what the type does. The enneagram is able to help people spot when they are being run by their passions, allowing people to satisfy their needs in a healthier manner.

For example, the passion for type seven happens to be gluttony. This is the traditional meaning for overeating which extends to over consumption. The people with this type look for experiences in trying to find a sense of fulfillment which they fear may remain elusive. In truth, they may feel that nothing they embark on will bring the fulfillment which they look for to bring happiness and contentment.

Enneagram as a self-discovery tool to benefit your life

The enneagram allows for one to get on a journey towards self-enlightenment and acceptance for who you are. Everyone has a basic driving force and a preferred strategy set for unique talents and strengths that make us individuals. We look at the world and the present era with specific perspectives and we are drawn in particular directions as individuals. These preferences can harden into modes of behavior, which also strangle the ways in which we grow. At times when people first discover the particular type they are, they might say that they would like to change to another type. That is an indication they are judging one type to be more desirable as compared to another. The key to utilizing the enneagram would be exploration without the use of judgment. The question is if each pattern provided a large reservoir of talent, which is equally valuable. You are undoubtedly growing and maturing everyday so there should not be a limit to the potentials irrespective of your type. Every evidence points to the fact that no enneagram type is better than the other. In each archetype there are different levels of maturity and generativity. The level of maturity may vary though in different contexts.

Each type of enneagram represents a deep habit. It shows a theme that for a lot of people is constant throughout their life, though the possibilities for the mental, physical or spiritual developments have no bounds. The type is a fundamental form of human habit. With some technology and coaching, it is possible to utilize the information gained from this information to transform patterns for more effective behavior and perspectives.

As we study our types, it begins to dawn on us that there is a range of healthy to unhealthy behaviors we engage in unwittingly. When we are relaxed, we may feel safe and have natural gifts that are inherent to our type that are at our disposal. Similarly, when under stress, we have ways of reacting that may run contrary to the best intentions we have. When triggered we may also react in the best way to protect ourselves from pain, fear or shame and respond so quickly that we do not even acknowledge the effect that it has on other people. When growing to understand our type, we develop the right skills which are particular to that type and that may allow us to reduce the levels of stress we harbor through reactivity and our quick responses which negatively affect the ones that are around us. This also allows the illustration of the greatest gifts and as we continue to learn, there is an understanding that others also have unconscious patterns and reactions which are predictable during times of crises, happening beyond the level of present awareness.

With more study, one may start to develop valuable traits such as compassion and understanding for themselves and others concerning the patterns of the type and then grow to appreciate just how fast any one can be triggered and how much it is not possible to note the patterns. Over the course of time it becomes easier to develop skills that would slow things down and bring us out of the trance that instilled patterns we engage. We can then become compassionate and sensitive to the emotional vulnerabilities of everyone and become skilled at holding space for them. Under stress, each category has a way they disconnect from their loved ones emotionally.

In depth exploration concerning the enneagram also assists one to navigate their relationships with more skill. Knowing the types of your family and colleagues can increase your understanding on their fears, defenses and motivations, allowing you to understand how they would interact with you and others. The other reason you should take this journey into self-exploration is the commitment to living a conscious and caring life though every day you may come across situations and people that could result in self-sabotaging reactions. Even if you had been on a spiritual path for some time, you may still be humbled by the manner that the unconscious reactions bring you to patterns that you had thought had been outgrown.

It could be that you tend to space when your spouse expresses painful emotions because it disrupts your carefree attitude, or you may turn to alcohol or other drugs when you feel like you are being shunned or things are not going your way. Irrespective of the pattern, everyone comes with habits that block self-expression and joy. All of these patterns which are negative cause their own suffering and they are linked to habits of the different enneagram types. Even in the event that you can recite deep spiritual truths when these patterns are triggered, you may still forget the bigger picture of who you are and the unique gifts that you can share with the world. The question then arises on how one can find clarity and free themselves from the fears, motivations and desires that fuel behavioral patterns and trigger other reactions from others.

Chapter 1: Three Structures, Wings Lines and Integration

Three centers

Human beings have three major ways of how they experience the world and that would be through thinking, feeling and sensation. The enneagram model and other mystical approaches considers three centers of intelligence along with perception of which mediate the life experiences that people have and their reactions to them. This corresponding to the heart, head and the body. From a psychological point of view, everyone utilizes the three centers. Everyone senses the environment and has an emotional reaction to it or thinks about things though each type may favor one of them as the main channel for the perception and response to incidences. The diagram then differentiates into three triads, which all correspond to one of the centers and the types within that are referred to as the head, heart and the body types. Each particular center has its own way of experiencing life and the negative emotion and concerns that are linked. The main types within each tried would be the ones that favor the particular center and reveal ways of dealing with that issue.

The nine-enneagram modes have been grouped into three centers, which include the heart, head and the body. While everyone has three centers, the personality type has a particular strength and a home base in one of them. The body center is inclusive of type 8, 9 and 1 which is formed as a response to anger. The head center has types 5, 6 and 7 that are created as a response to fear or anxiety and the heart center has types 3, 2 and 4 which is formed as a response to shame and a self-image formed. Understanding of One's primary center provides a significant key towards the development of personal and professional potential by overcoming the blind spots.

The three centers within a person interact with each other and one cannot work on one center without actually affecting the other two. As a matter of fact the center, which the enneagram type resides, is the psyche that people are least able to function freely as the function has been blocked by the ego. For example, the enneagram type nine, which is the body center, is the enneagram type which is mostly disengaged with the body, not physically speaking but internally.

Considering there are many sets of three in the enneagram of personality, there are also several ways in which to unpack the whole enneagram in bite size chunks of three. It may take some time to absorb some of the complex data and you might not get it incorporated on the first try. That is part of its charm as the enneagram is always new and surprising, concerning its nuances of insight upon insight, which proceed to evolve over the course of time. If you use the enneagram for the purposes of just becoming a number and to forgive and explain bad habits, then that is missing the point. The point would be to utilize the enneagram as the platform for self-discovery and personal growth. After decades of study and witnessing, the enneagram will enable you to unveil your innermost self and secrets.

The body center

This center houses types 8, 9 and 1 as mentioned before and these have distortions in their instincts, the root of life force and vitality. The body center entails intelligence of the body, which is a direct experience of our existence. That being a sense of life, connecting with yourself and having communication with other things. When you are not present, you lose your sense of confidence, existing and fullness. The major emotion for the body center would be anger. This usually comes from an instinctual response pertaining to the sense of interference or being messed with. The unconscious fear is concerning unity and this is where people may lose themselves, their functioning or not being intact. The body center needs autonomy and it is concerned about the influence on the surroundings.

As such, a type 8 may tend to act out their anger or express it very easily or in a rapid manner. They may also place their guard up very quickly in such a manner that no one can get to them or hurt their feelings. Their anger can come from a number of situations where they or another individual experiences injustice.

The head center

This is where the thinking takes place as well as analysis, remembrance and the projection of ideas about what other people and events ought to be. The head based types include 5, 6 and 7 and they may respond to existence through the use of their thoughts. They may also have vivid imaginations and there is a strong ability to correlate and analyze ideas. Even those who are very gregarious claim they are very satisfied with the company that is brought by their own thoughts. For those types, thinking represents a way for the pre-empting of fear.

The mind has to keep all of its defenses and come up with a dissociated sense of yourself and produce a sense of direction. The main emotion when it comes to the head center would be fear. When you can experience the presence and stillness in a direct manner, you experience it as the ground of everything. That knowledge is the basis of faith. When you lose the ground of support and guidance, you may become panicky and fearful. The head center type needs security and they're concerned with beliefs and strategy. A type 5 may react to fear through retreating to their mind and so reducing personal needs. There is a need for example to master something in order to feel safe and to observe surroundings in order to make an analysis concerning what is going on. The type 6s respond to fear as well through considering what may happen in the worst case scenario. Usually, they could be ready for anything that may go wrong. They can look for guidance from those who are in charge in order to deal with no guidance issues or they can rebel against the said authorities when they become dependent. The type 7s as well react to fear through trying to turn awkward or uncomfortable situations into something which is exciting and new in order to avoid the feelings of fear. They may fear being trapped in pain, grief or anxiety and go into an activity that helps them escape or keeps them otherwise occupied.

The heart center

This is the place where people experience emotions or the sensations that tell people the way they feel as opposed to what they think about something. Emotions of the heart can range from the dramatic and the wrong to the most subtle or mute feelings. People overall feel connected to other people within this center but also have a yearning for fulfillment and love. They include the types 2, 3 and 4 these groups have distortions concerning their feelings. The heart is aware of the truth and it lets us know things such as identity and the truth of who we are. It is also where people derive a sense of meaning and glory about their existence. When a person says something that is resonating and true, the heart will be in agreement and you might feel connected to the message and to the person. As such, being in touch with the heart shows the quality of existence and shows how to know the truth. Another common emotion when it comes to the heart center would be shame. The types 2, 3 and 4 are in search for recognition, validation and mirroring. This is needed because when you are young, there is a limited capacity for self-reflection. You can only ascertain who you are through the perspectives of others. As such, when you do not get the attention that you would like there is some shame, deficiency and a sense of emptiness. The head centers want a lot of attention and are concerned with the way they are portrayed or their self-image.

The type twos can be caring for others in order to get good rapport and so they do not feel a sense of shame. They can create an image of being needed or likeable, though they have issues knowing what they need or feel. They often know this when there are a lot of people that are dependent on them for survival. Type Threes are very out of touch with their inner selves and believe they need positive feedback and affirmations from other people. They can find value and self-worth through performance in order to avoid the feelings of shame that could come about. They also try and project images of success into the community and look for the admiration of others in order to fuel their self-image.

The type fours may usually look for the reasons why they are unique when compared to other people. They initiate and sustain moods and use emotions as a means through which they can defend against being rejected. This is done through the dramatization of their hurts and losses, causing them to avoid deeper feelings and get attention or pity from other people. As such, the type twos externalize shame and create images of a great individual, the type threes feel conflict considering they have a lot of shame and cover this with an image of success. The type fours manage to internalize their shame and have initiated an image which illustrates their identity.

How the Enneagram centers work

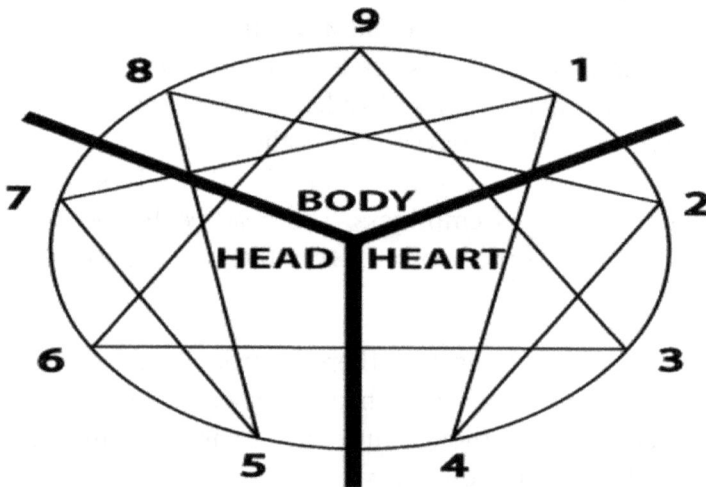

A lot can be said concerning the way personality develops in the Enneagram. Each type may favor one center though everyone contains and is affected by the heart, head and the body centers within themselves in different ways. The enneagram is descriptive concerning different qualities of the centers for all human beings, which is a structure that is common to everyone, this then illustrating how this manifests differently for the various modes.

There are 'two of us' inside all, which is the essential self-known and the personality that believes itself to be that of the individual. Of the two selves, the personality tends to manifest through habitual narrow modes of thought and survival reactions. These are referred to as passion, fixation and instinctual subtypes and they are the source of repetition within our daily lives. Describing of the essential self, heart and the head allows for a holy opposite which is a particular aspect of essence. These are known as the holy virtue and holy idea. The idea of virtue and the holy idea are more like holy seeds as opposed to holy opposites, considering they are with everyone at birth and name the divine qualities of the soul. People just forgot this as they learnt to deal with the world and developed personality defense structures. The personality masks and protects the essential self and it also does an imitation like a mirror that is reflecting back to front through looking for the forgotten aspects in the outside world instead of within. This would be the basis of differences between the nine types. In summary; one of the underlying structures for the types is that they have nine distinct ways of manifestation. For each of the nine, their spiritual qualities and psychological self seem to narrow their focus towards the attention of trying to imitate the innate forgotten qualities within their type.

The head center: fixation and holy idea

The fixation would be an indication of the personality's habitual pre-occupation or the focus of their attention. It may be described as the metaphorical hamster in the mental wheel. The holy idea on the other hand shows a state of awareness which is experienced rather than thought of by the spiritual head center at the time that it is free of the fixation.

The heart center: passion and holy virtue

The habitual underlying emotion of the heart center is known as Passion. Early Christians had known this aspect being one of the nine interruptions to the life of prayer as stated by Evagrius Ponticus. At the present, they correspond to the seven deadly sins added to fear and deceit. The essential state of being experienced in the heart is known as Holy Virtue, otherwise referred to as the virtue of essence.

The body center

The word subtypes means three survival instincts which are connected to the body center for the enneagram. Survival, which is the matter of life and death, is considered in the last resort through unconscious gut reaction and instinct. The nine fixations and passions define the personality attributes and they can be recognized as 'what a person does'. The subtypes define three different means of manifesting each type, this causing the behavior from them to be believed as a matter of life or death.

These instincts concern survival in fundamental areas such as:

1. Self-preservation, which is the right to exist with the energy focusing on material wellbeing.
2. There is a social consideration of the right to belong since human beings are tribal people. Survival is dependent on acceptance within the tribe.
3. There are sexual needs as everyone has the right to be loved. This is also related to the instinct to survive through what is

newly created in one on one relationships irrespective of whether that is a baby or validation by another person.

Everyone tends to focus on one of these, depending on their experience towards the greatest threat to their essential self as they grew up. This includes whether people were fed, were warm, nurtured well, accepted by the family and their attempts to attract unconditional love. At the present there is some debate as whether the subtype focus is present from the time of birth, regardless of whether it is developmental and a result of the environment or a combination of the two just in the same way as an individual's adult persona is. In either case the result is while all three centers are important for happy functioning in life, one of them is going to be seen unconsciously as the greatest source of pain or threat. This then draws a lot of energy and attention to it and looks to be one of the greatest sources of happiness and satisfaction.

How the enneagram works

The enneagram is a tool for great subtlety though the central is based upon what happens to be quite simplistic. That is that the personality was developed in order to protect our higher self and is linked inseparably to it. There is a simple observation which allows the use of this knowledge and it is not unique to the Enneagram. We are consistent of two people. The first is the soul or the essence. It is neither thought, feeling or sensation yet it's the person. The other is the personality that identifies itself with thoughts, feelings and sensations. Most of the time, it is confused for the true self but it can be changed.

The difference between the spiritual and psychological nature is only just apparent. Both of them are integral to the people that we are. While being alive, there is a need for a personality in order to mediate between the higher selves and the world in order to assist in getting things done but there is also a need to recognize its nature. The personality represents a set of tools which help us through life while other parts do not assist very much. Though you might have adopted them in order to keep you safe, by the time you become an adult, they become part of the negative problems.

In order to change or transcend, the first thing that one has to know is what the problem is. If you want to make a journey it would be first helpful to create the journey as it helps in having a map of the terrain to know where you are on the map and what obstacles that you may come across. This is a big part towards the value of the Enneagram. It represents a map of the particular terrain. In the same manner that traversing the Sahara would not require one to pack snow climate gear, if your go-to habit is fear, then it will not help to work on anger and pride. Envy is a big issue for some people while anger is for others and so forth.

When it comes to essence, the higher self, and the mystical arts describe the attributes of the soul. The spiritual gifts and the essence of each of the nine types of the enneagrams are variations of being, consciousness and bliss. When you get presence, then you find that all three centers are united and the three gifts avail themselves.

The head center for one corresponds to the visualization center allegedly used in Buddhist meditations and a number of the practices that relate to Ignatian spirituality. The head center knows what is real and trusts it. That is to say that Christianity is trustworthy. This then relates to faith as it needs no proof because it only knows what is true and discerns the significance of what is in the unique time. This discernment lets us perceive the way that the world works and gives us wisdom in order to act in a courageous manner in harmony with the requirements of the world.

The head is the spiritual heart center opened in the Sufi and Christian practices. The liturgy, devotional prayer and changing all provided access to the spiritual heart. In the west, the heart is associated with love while in the enneagram; the concept of love which is unconditional belongs to the belly. This is a given and it is where people come from or who they are and where they return. The yearning for what is known as love is actually an outward movement for the soil and the urge to unite. The heart types know that it is about the relationships and the unfolding time and space because of the interweaving. The heart wants to reach out and respond and create something new when it comes to hope. The belly center finally has almost been forgotten in the west as an organ of spiritual perceptions. It is correspondent to the concept that is known as hara in Japan and is the focus of all practices that are rooted in Zen. Love exists as a necessary part for creation. The gifts of the belly center would have to do with the nature of reality of being and of presence.

According to Gurdieff, it is possible to identify the chief features as most of the work has been accomplished and the Enneagram allows for this to happen. The inner self differentiates between essence and personality and that would be the key towards spiritual growth. Through the means of self-observation it is possible to recognize the automatic reactions of the personality and then use them as the reminders for the qualities that we have. In that way, it then becomes possible to regain the ability to respond to life from a perspective which is not biased and in tune with the true self. If you are skilled, then the inner self may assist in realizing patterns and bring out the unused and hidden potentials. Knowledge of particular terrain makes the efforts that much easier and accurate. It is not a query for transcending or subduing the personality, but rather befriending it and learning the manner that it points us to. Irrespective of whether people approach the personal growth as spiritual or both, it's completely up to them. People are able to understand their background influences or mediate for long periods of time every day. Unless it increases the humane-ness and loving kindness and unless daily actions and thoughts are harmonious and creative, then it is not growth.

Wings lines and integration

The enneagram is more than the nine types or points as represented on an intersection of a triangle. It is one of the psychodynamic frameworks which gives a strong model for understanding the manner in which integration and development work. It does not necessarily give a quick fix with a limited lifespan once there is insight. It allows individuals to develop themselves over the course of time as it proceeds to speak to us and the circumstances that continue to change. In the framework though, instincts, wings and the levels of integration are representative of the movement and journey that we are following in life.

The wings concern adjacent types to the core type on the enneagram circle. These neighbors may influence but they do not alter the core type. If the core type is like ice cream, then the wing would indicate the sauce that you can add to your ice cream, so to speak. That is not a second type of ice cream that you can add to the ice cream, it is just the flavor of the adjacent type. Everyone has access to both of their winds and each has a different set of resources and attributes that can be helpful at different times. Sometimes one of these wings proves to be more predominant and familiar. Some individuals do not like to add too much sauce to the wings, metaphorically speaking, while others like to balance it out. The wings are there to enable people to understand the types not in isolation but via their relationship to each other. Considering the types of the enneagram are viewed as a continuum, one's wings can assist with understanding the subtleties of one's core type. Through leaning into your wings from one side or the other, it becomes possible to expand your perspective and increase emotional and behavioral repertoires. The wings could also give a way to understand tensions and the effects on a person when they are stuck and then initiate the potential to reframe the situation as a point at which they can be able to develop into something more.

The gift of the enneagram is when it comes to potential and movement that flexes between the core, line of release and the apparent connection. There is an obvious question for those who are acquainting themselves with the enneagram as to whether people are just one type or a combination of two or more. The appropriate response is both yes and no obviously.

The enneagram is a dynamic framework, which is to state that it isn't restricted to one place on the figure. Individuals move around to the next enneagram which focuses on relying upon their necessities and specific conditions. While the fundamental personality remains the command post, we also invest some energy occupying or visiting a portion of the other personality types. This is definitely not an irregular procedure. The enneagram figure is demonstrative of the examples that every one of the personality types follow. Since the image is somewhat striking, when individuals originally go over the enneagram they may think about whether the lines imply anything. They are significant as the lines follow the courses that you travel when you experience distinctive moves in mindfulness and conduct in your day by day presence. You go along these lines from one point to the next and now and again you may return, moving forward at a quicker rate, barely seeing the move with regards to the viewpoint. On different occasions, you may have a more sensational move or even invest some energy in a point instead of the basic personality type.

It would appear there is some inalienable association of knowledge inside the chart. In this way, the enneagram is unique in relation to the next personality modes. There are different frameworks which offer a depiction of four or even sixteen types. However, the enneagram is something other than a basic rundown. It is an all-encompassing thing that is based by the arithmetic and symmetry of this graph returning a large number of years. With regards to people, however, the lines convey vital data concerning mental examples. Pieces of the lessons concerning the enneagram is somewhat mysterious. You may ask how the lines inside the graph can work as an indicator for the conduct of others in day by day life. There is by all accounts zero logical confirmation that all things are considered. The answer can be learnt through testing the hypothesis and checking whether it has down to earth esteem. One may have the capacity to see in your life certain examples as given by the lines which are in the chart. Seeing that it has been utilized by thousands amid the ages, there is by all accounts somewhat of an accord that these lines mean something or they allude to something which is unmistakable.

Lines of the diagram

THE PEACEMAKER
9

THE CHALLENGER 8

1 THE REFORMER

THE ENTHUSIAST 7

2 THE HELPER

THE LOYALIST 6

3 THE ACHIEVER

THE INVESTIGATOR 5

4 THE INDIVIDUALIST

► Arrow line points to disintegration
— Non-arrow line points to integration

There is a body inside the training that has customarily used the graph as a means for understanding the standards administering the universe like the events of phenomena and how they move in designs. The investigation was based by the properties of numbers and the usage of instinct as it started before the logical revelations of the ongoing occasions. Inside the cutting edge period, the examples of vitality might be evaluated or considered in manners which are more exact. However a few ideas including quantum material science conflict with the breaking points of the examinations as of now. There might be a lot of meta designs which have not been evaluated up until now also.

Amid the prior occasions, masterminds and researchers have taken a stab at clarifying the characteristic world utilizing graphs and numbers like the enneagram. While there is no featuring of that use of the enneagram in the present discourse about personality, there are a couple of numerical components that can help in the investigation of individuals.

When you take a gander at the nine pointed graph, it will end up obvious, there are covering sets of lines. One of them would be the triangle joining the points 3, 6 and 9. This internal triangle demonstrates the law of three that is there in both mainstream and religious settings. In the Christian religion, there are ideas that identify with the quantity of three, for example, the trinity of God, the Son and the Holy Spirit. In the mainstream world, the law of three can be depicted as the postulation, absolute opposite and the union. As indicated by the cutting edge father of the enneagram Gurdjieff, who conveyed the enneagram to the west in 1915 and presented the idea in this way. Point three would be the place for the commencement of vitality. Point three is noted as the place of opposing and the improvement of vitality or blessed denying while point nine would be the place of interceding and the harmonization of vitality. The interesting thing concerning this issue is that the personality types that are related with these points hope to encapsulate something concerning these traits. Threes have a starting and going ahead component. The points sixes for the most part consider it for quite a while and consider advancement of the thought further to get the wrinkles out and to think of a refined arrangement. Nines are professedly individuals that look for equalization and concordance. They are the individuals who are mediators. You can now and again portray personality types 3, 6 and 9 as displaying the characteristics for no, perhaps and yes. The lines inside the internal triangle interface the personality types. In the following area, the content will consider the manner in which they move forward and backward from a point to another amid various occasions.

Regardless, there is something, which is very valuable about the possibility of threes. Keeping in mind the end goal to start another venture, there is the requirement for enough inspiration and starting vitality. In spite of the fact that to an extent we know things generally don't go ahead in a straight line and instead appears in work for personal development. There is obstruction all the time regarding something in ourselves or the condition that should be countered. If you can draw in this arrangement of deterrents in a way which is wise to see it as a helpful piece of the procedure, the first arrangement or the aim advances into something that is significantly more fruitful. The other method to see this on the off chance that you can have a decent discussion or gainful clash between the starting parts and the opposing parts is you move to some goals or amalgamation. In spite of the fact that without that procedure, activities or people would not form or develop into something which is better. The other arrangement of the lines inside the enneagram would be the one associating the points 4, 2, 1, 8, 5, 7. This can be used so as to show the law of seven which is a number set that is connected with the seven notes in the regular melodic scale. While the law of three concerns the characteristics of vitality or three types of power at work, the law of seven concerns the movement for vitality and the movements of steps towards each task or action. There are individuals that have observed the law of seven to be very helpful in the arranging of their exercises to ensure a specific end goal. As of now, it is just conceivable to see how this arrangement of lines and the connections between the numbers inside the set advise the investigation of the personality types. In the event that you happen to separate 1 by the number 7 you then get something which is repeating from the decimal.. The hypothesis of the enneagram proposes that personality types inside the numbers 1, 4, 2, 8, 5 and 7 tend to move forward and backward thusly relying upon some interior conditions.

Wing points and dynamic points of movement

There are two methods of movement that exist on the enneagram. Every one of them has distinctive characteristics in this way. One of them concerns the movement around the periphery of the hover points delineated on each side of the personality type. The adjacent points as specified before are the wing points. The other is the movement inside the enneagram to the two points that are associated with one's point by the straight lines. These are what are alluded to as the 'Dynamic Points'. These points are the nearby neighbors and one can visit them since they are ideally adjacent. It doesn't take a considerable measure to move and embrace a viewpoint and the personal perspective of the wing points. In spite of the fact that they are distinctive modes from your own particular, you can undoubtedly see the world through their eyes or go up against their conduct either positively or negatively. At the point when people are finding their sort, they may relate to some wing points. Truly, a few people could see themselves similarly with the two neighboring types. However they may not know which one is the essential kind.

It may be the case that the purpose behind this is each type can be portrayed as a mix of the two wing points. For one, in the event that you happen to mix a nine alongside a two then you may think of what has all the earmarks of being a one. Additionally, on the off chance that you mix a four and a six then you may think of a five. Individuals approach both of their wings. Every one of them has an alternate arrangement of assets and characteristics which might be used as a portion of the time. In say this there is proof that one of these wings is transcendent or a commonplace. One may watch themselves with a specific end goal to find that they have a prevalent wing, or you may encounter moving to the two wings on an equivalent premise. In any examples that hold, it is clear the fundamental personality type can be influenced by the nearness of the wings which at that point prompts noteworthy fluctuations in conduct and viewpoint among the nine classes.

As opposed to moving to the wing points, the movement inside the enneagram isn't that simple and can be a critical move in the experience of our lives. They are named as psychodynamic or even dynamic considering the personality experiences noteworthy changes. You may likewise be in an alternate point of view and style of conduct. You and other people who are a major part of your life will come to know about these progressions. There are times these movements are befuddling and irritating just as they were occurring outside of a man's control. In spite of the fact when mindful of these movements, you can oversee them sufficiently and they can be productive for personal and expert advancements. It seems as though you approach another arrangement of assets and it is a set which includes esteem or makes the expected equalization to the standard personality type. The movement of these dynamic points can help with venturing out of the limits and extending the choices sufficiently. It additionally implies to not getting stuck inside the habitual style of response to the environment. Whether you are on the inner triangle or on another set of lines, there may be two lines which connect the personality type to two other points. However, each line presents a different quality and direction to it. In one of the directions, such as the forward directions, there is the resource point. This is the point where you can access a quality which would provide some assistance to taking action in the world. There are a number of enneagram teachers that name this as the stress point considering whether you go there and when you're under a significant amount of stress, accessing the competencies and intelligences of this point. Both claims are true though the stress point has a negative type of connotation that you are using the term 'the resource point'. This is not necessarily a negative thing though it can be a bit uncomfortable.

In the other direction, moving backwards provides the relaxation or the heart point. When you go towards that direction, you move to inhabit personality modes which are considered to be valuable for transformation and personal growth. That point is key to a number of the underlying issues within the personality of an individual as the undeveloped side of the self. It is as if you have to relax and let down the normal defenses of the normal way of seeing the world to become flexible as well as vulnerable to others and situations. When you feel safe and secure, you can then go deeper within yourself to learn more about who you are and become available to loved ones. Obviously coming to terms with some of these core issues and feelings within the relaxation point may be a bit challenging. There is a propensity for one to snap to their usual personal type and its perspective and standard practices. On the other hand, if you have the ability to stay long enough within the relaxation point to integrate various lessons then there is a possibility to re-inhabit the personality type with more balance and integration.

As such in the enneagram, you move toward the resource point which in this manner; 3 would go to 9 then 6 then 3 and so on. It may also go to the other set of lines where 1 goes to 4 then 2 then 8 then 5 then 7 then 1. Going to the relaxation point means backwards within the opposite direction. That would then become clearer as you go through the personality types as provided within the book.

Point One: Wing points

At the point when the ninth wing is predominant, the Ones are more arranged toward amicability and equalization. That involves the drive to get things right which is intervened by a longing to be agreeable. They would then be able to end up quieter and go at a slower pace. A potential drawback to these wings is it can make the Ones set in their ways which is less versatile or adaptable to the desires for different people or the requirements for the occasion. One preferred standpoint to this wing is the way to be beneficial inside a methodological or relentless way, while keeping consideration to rightness and quality.

At the point when the wing is predominant, the Ones are drawn toward associations with different people. Doing the correct things at the present implies additionally being strong and supportive. With this wing being dynamic, the Ones are more expressive and ground breaking. A potential drawback here would be nervousness or being vexed which originates from interpersonal clashes or the feeling that other individuals are not getting things done in the correct way. One favorable position to the wing is it would make it potentially viable as a blend for individuals association aptitudes. The assignment for the production of request and the correct outcomes would be centered more around the general population, instead of the material items.

Dynamic Points

The unwinding point for the Ones would be point Seven. Instead of looking to locate the one right away, the Ones may open up to new potential outcomes. It is less demanding for one to endure numerous plans and choices. They happen to be less incredulous of themselves and other individuals. At the point when the Ones begin to unwind into Seven, they can begin to shed a portion of the physical pressure so it is less demanding for them to have a great time and simply run with things. On the off chance that the unwinding point isn't incorporated in the correct way, it is conceivable that Ones can 'carry on' if the typical poise isn't there. They could result to eating or drinking too much. Despite the fact that when they prevail in the combination of the two points, there could be some enthusiasm and positive feeling of Seven which implants the obligation and diligent work of the One. Spontaneity and flexibility are acclimatized with intentionality and uprightness.

The resource point for Ones would be point four. This is normally where they would connect with being disturbed. The weakness however is there is a sentiment of stress in tough situations this creating emotions that may turn out as being excessively disordered or even forceful.

Point Two: Wing points

The way that the twos express themselves is balanced through an innate feeling to do things the right way. On the advantageous side, they happen to be more reserved and so they control themselves in ways where they show off their skills. They also happen to be thoughtful and balance aspects of self-control with the levels of their emotions to come out with a better assessment of scenarios. The bad thing with this combination of attributes is it can result in duality of natures which then leads to physical tension. They can become uncomfortable if they become too self-critical if everything has to be in its order. Self-containment that is with the One wing and the warmth and outgoing of Two initiates outgoing energy of Two which leads to stability and relative effectiveness.

When Three wing is predominant, then the Two might utilize their skill in order to consider the requirements of others in order to become more successful in their professions. They are very responsive. To a particular point, they are able to match Threes in every detail when it comes to working toward the objective. However, they are not Threes and over the course of time, they are going to have to slow things down. When the Three wing is active, the Two will make good performers. On the other hand, that particular wing point will make things harder over time to bring their attention to their needs, doubts and personal agendas.

Dynamic point

The Two then moves to the point four which is the place of relaxation and calm. As opposed to the usual paying attention to others to initiate a sense of security, at this place attention is drawn to their needs. They are at this point able to feel their emotions. The disadvantage is unlike others. Like the Fours, they may get stuck in depression which is maintained by seeing only what is missing in a particular relationship be it at work or within their social circles. Their skills though are to center inside oneself and to know what they want or to develop a sort of emotional intelligence, empowering the capacity of Twos for teamwork and networking. Being with point Four can assist them to find a home within themselves. In another direction, the point Eight would be the point of resource for these Twos. Irrespective of whether it is productive they may depend on how the Twos are able to manage the assertive energy that is at Point eight. The question is whether they reach this point in a calm manner or whether they go off the rails. There are Twos that naturally just combine the going forward energy which is in their type with the assertion and taking charge energy that is found in the Eight. There are others who have a hard time going to Eight unless there is stress from the outside. Some access to point eight is good for learning to handle conflict, which usually does not come very easy.

Point three: wing designations

When the Two wing is predominant, then the Threes can be hospitable. They may bring their focus to networking in order to further their work. Successful connections made with other individuals are just a part of their program towards productivity. The Threes can display more people skills as compared to what be associated with those who are point Twos. They can sustain contact for a long time beyond a lot of personality modes in the enneagram.

The problem is the way that both points reinforce dependency for the external approvals, trying to get recognized, which may create vanity.

Dynamic points

The relaxation stage for the point Threes is Six. This is where they feel like they can open space for introspection. For all of them, especially when they are in places of leadership, the skill is to pose queries and understand opposing forces. This comes from point Six and is needed for success in the long term along with effectiveness. Point Six takes on objectives and encourages informed decision making.

Point four wing points

When the Three wing is predominant, the Fours will then consider the external environment. They have the ability to work with Threes in order to achieve a good amount of success in their business operations. They are able to place aside a lot of individualism to blend in, while still keeping personalized touches within their presentation. They can meet the expectations of others but they will usually feel tension concerning their social life and public representation. When the Five wing is predominant then the four will seek tasks which have time for them to introspect.

Dynamic points

The point of relaxation for the Fours would be point One. When they are feeling appreciated then the gravity would shift to the body center. They get very calm emotionally at this point. They do not have a lot of mood swings. The feelings of sadness and longing transforms into the One point which is backed by a sense of practical activity. The point Fours would like to pace things that are right, rather than consider what is wrong. The resource point for the Fours would be point Two. The Fours usually say that it is stressful to stay in this forward moving point for a long time. It can begin to feel pretentious as if they feel like they are giving up individuality to win approval and make personal connection. The Fours are able to accept they are going out of their comfort zone to an external setting that would work better as opposed to feeling forced to socialize.

Point five wing point

When the point Four wing is predominant then the Fives have an active emotional lifestyle. Even though the emotions can be hard to see, they are still quite valid and this places a direct influence on behavior. The challenge would be integration of feeling functions, so they are not pulling in different directions or creating tension. While the Four wing can support interpersonal warmth, it may also lead to disjointed styles. When the Sixth wing is the predominant one, the activity of the mental center is the one which is reinforced. There happens to be strong focus on technical data here with systems of information as the solution to life issues. The problem is that the Fives are prone to worry which threatens problems to be larger than they actually are.

Dynamic points

Point Eight is the relaxation point. Quiet and withdrawn, the individual may become body centered and even excessive in the way they express themselves. Both the Eight and the Five points are self-referencing and so it is not easy for one to hear or include the feelings of another person. Though, it comes with a lot of good energy if managed in the right manner. The resource point for the Five is point seven. On the other hand, point Seven allows the Five to be more outgoing. They can become the life of the party when their enthusiasm is engaged.

Point six wing points

When the Five wing is the predominant one, then the Sixes are going to want to keep their privacy as the main priority. They might be a bit reserved in social situations unless they know the people who are there. They also have a tendency to want to know everything about a scenario before taking action. The Seven wing on point Six ,propels the Sixes toward participation in experiences which are enjoyable. In the same manner as the Sevens, they can create plans and options provided where they are unaware of what the limits are.

Dynamic points

The relaxation point for the Sixes is point Nine. That would be illustrated when they drop their gravity center to the belly. They have a habit of scanning their surroundings in order to anticipate problems, finding out what risks are present. The point Three is the resource point for the Sixes. This allows the Sixes the chance of achieving actions more immediately than usual for their personality type. As opposed to being guided by rules, the Three energy is responsive and adaptable.

Point seven wing point

When the Six wing is the predominant one the Sevens get reinforced. They may become engrossed in everything that is going on that they rarely pay attention to their wellbeing. They also have the capacity to plan and visiualise with a lot of mental speed. When the Eighth wing is the predominant one, then the Sevens get pulled to more physical experiences. They may become very good adventurers even if it concerns business ventures, partying or sports. The expansive nature of both points can make them a bit restless and have them doing things that make them feel relevant.

Dynamic points

The relaxation point for point Seven would be point Five. The interesting thing is that when the sevens feel they are safe and secure they are able to remediate to their attention style of up and out. They may retreat within themselves and become very reflective. However a lot of Sevens understand there is big benefit in being able to center inside of oneself in order to quiet the mind and to think in a clear manner, withdrawing from the flow of activity. The resource point for point Sevens is point One. Because the Sevens are usually situated in a position of being okay when others are okay, their point allows them to be critical, causing their actions to have to be done in the right manner. When they are placed in this position by the stress they experience, they may exhibit attributes of point One, like being judgmental and resentful.

Point eight wing points

When Seven is the predominant one, the Eight can be a charming individual and very outgoing. They tend to embrace adventure and risk at this situation. They also have a lot of access to vitality and even aggression. This energy can enable them to be very good at business or contracting. In contrast, the Nine wing allows the eights to be laid back. They can exercise strength and control at this stage. Their energy is usually much quieter as compared to the other Eights that may give the impression that they are not aggressive in the first case.

Dynamic points

The Two is the relaxation point for the Eight. At this juncture, they are able to adequately access their emotions; which is not very easy for the Eight. To a certain point the Eight has concentrated their assertion and defenses to consider a world filled with a lot of conflict, it entails courage to open up to be seen as being vulnerable. The emotions of people can be hidden in the right way, releasing energy and allowing for a lot of motivation for better or worse.

The resource point for point Eight is point Five. This is a go-to point for the Eights that look for privacy on a daily basis. They also need their own space and instead of their mode of going into activity, the Five just allows them to strategize and go into quiet reflection. The Eight may over invest in a lot of things, meaning a bit of detachment may be quite helpful to them. Though if they stay too long at this point, they can then become shut down and melancholic.

Point Nine wing points

When Eight is the predominant wing, the Nine can adopt attributes which are very methodical and exact from others around them. The Nines with a One wing are going to feel motivated to go along with the expectations of the Ones that are in authority. They will just not keep up with the compliance in the same thorough manner as the ones and they may forget or act out in a passive aggressive manner. The other predominant wing for the Nine is the Eight which brings the Nine into their rebellious side. With this wing, the Nine can be more assertive as compared to their cousins with the One wing.

Dynamic points

The Three is the point of relaxation. At this time, the Nine can be in a more active feeling area. This can be overwhelming which allows the Nines to derive questions about who they are and what their true identities are. The resource point though for the Nine would be the Six. When the Nine becomes motivated by events that are outside their control, they go to this point. Their perception becomes much sharper and instead they are able to zero in on what the problem is at the time.

Chapter Two: Personality Types

People vary physically, meaning you can distinguish one person from the other through various features such as their skin complexions, their hair, their height, their weight, and their shapes amongst others. That said, we could classify them further and group those who share these traits together and give them names as we did blonds, blacks, white, and tall.

The same way we classify people with their physical attributes we can classify them with their individual and particular personalities. There is a reason why the world is as it is, why we attain certain achievements in life, why we excel in different areas in life, why we handle situations as we do, why some relationships last and some don't, why we handle pain differently and why some people are more social than others. Our personalities, determine a lot in a person because the shape our attitudes towards different stimuli in our environments. This eventually alters our approach and reactions to such circumstances.

Personalities are the people we are or rather the kind of personality we possess and this affects the way we relate to each other. For example you meet a person covered in tattoos and dreadlocks. One person may assume they are immoral individuals with no respect for religion and therefore dangerous. Another person may think that its rather impressive, attractive and that he or she has an artistic and creative personality. These different reactions are drawn because of the different personalities within us. This can also apply in our relationships, normally unlike people attract and end up having amazing relationships and this is where people will say "opposites attract". However, imagine a case where no one was different or special?.. What you stand for is what the next person stands for and the other and the other. Naturally this would bore you to death, listening to the same songs, loving the same things, doing the same careers, having the same opinions and so on. At first this all sounds so interesting and fun but if you contextualize it and put it into perspective, you realize that with time it becomes overwhelming and boring. Then there would be no point of conversing because no different ideologies are being exchanged just the same old things redundantly. This would kill so many relationships as there is no excitement or exploration of different perspectives between people and life. This challenging no purpose and no fulfillment, just reciprocity everywhere, meaning itself would be lost in life.

Another area that will be affected by this is our careers because we are moved by the same stimuli pushing us into wanting to achieve the same goals which isn't necessarily a bad thing but can lead to stagnation as there are so many areas in life that need to be tapped into and exploited. We all have a purpose in life and that's what makes some of us politicians, chefs, bankers and others entrepreneurs.

We are pushed by different things and moved by different stimuli leading us to our destined paths, where we are also pushed differently to achieve or reach different levels of our chosen paths. That is the reason why some end up in management, some stagnate, some starts rival businesses and some opt out and choose different paths in life.

Our personalities shape our thinking, attitudes, perceptions, beliefs and behaviors. They make us who we are. They make life what it is.

There are various groupings of personalities and they are grouped together because of their strongest traits or the one thing about them that stands out most. We'll look at each of the Nine groupings and how it affects the people towards relations, success, purpose and overall approach what they face in life.

Type 1: The Perfectionist

The perfectionist, just as their name suggests, they are always keeping it 100. In whatever aspect of life, they do it to the best of their ability, they take life very seriously and whatever tasks the take on they either do it perfectly or don't do it at all. With type Ones, there in no in-between.. They are honest, dependable and use common sense. What this basically means is that they will make great efforts in straightening the conditions around them. Whatever seems off they would go extra miles to put it back to how it should be even if it is a small change to something.

The challenge comes when their point of view isn't attainable or when what they are trying to change cannot be changed. This drives a hole through them because they are idealistic and believe that everything should be complete and in perfect accuracy. This is a big challenge that affects their perceptions and attitudes towards different aspects of their lives.

For example, in relationships they might try to make their partners see things as they do and try making them have a common point of view with them towards everything. This, in most cases, would make them vulnerable to being prideful and might come off as rude or arrogant possibly leading them to poor relationships and interactions. The ability to take and receive information willingly from different parties is what makes communication and relations what they are and adds meat to the bone. Having a strong minded individual who has strong beliefs about what he knows can be very frustrating at times and can drive away interest or lead to arguments that are pointless, especially if they are wrong.

Their purpose in life in general can also have its fair share of effects from their personality. By this I mean that because they do not accept less than perfect and struggle taking others' opinions they might end up wasting their time, money and energy into trying to prove facts that are nonexistent. Causing them to chase dead causes and since they don't share freely, end up suffering emotionally and psychologically, keeping all of their hurt within themselves and refusing to share.

It isn't all bad though because their perfectionist nature serves them well at most times as they tend to be honest and responsible, meaning they often try and get their facts right and raise the standards of those around them. They take full responsibility of their actions, making them reliable people to turn to for advice because they tend to see reality for what it is; right from wrong, good from bad and black from white. Their clarity is essential in life and offers a clear perspective of their journey, allowing them to assess what works and what doesn't work. This is a very important tool in life because life is all about improving and working on your flaws while dropping what doesn't work to attain the end product of being we intend or wish to be.

Type 2: The Giver

The second personality is the Giver, I can call them the "fit in" crew, since they like to seek human approval from amongst those they interact with. To them, approval is of utmost importance even if means making personal sacrifices on different things in their life. This personality is cautious of everything they say and can be good individuals to nurture and guide as they try seeing things from your perspective, accommodating or welcoming your thoughts, therefore giving you great advice and opinions on life. This though comes at a cost because having nothing you stand for can make you lose your identity as a person even if it benefits the other parties. The givers are very caring and they like to make sure everyone is 'okay' especially their friends and family. And also this is a very good trait, they can sometimes get stuck in situations where they believe everyone is selfish, however they made need to realize that they themselves need to be a little more selfish.

This affects different aspects of their lives, for example work, friendships and their relationships. They are very loving and accommodating people and the fact that they actually take time to know you and understand things as you see them, means that they are very good people to relate to. work with and have as friends. As said before this can have a down side where they may depend on people's approval. Lack of approval can then lead them to going into breakdowns and losing self-esteem, lowering their confidence in what they offer or bring to the table.

Independence of thought and having something you stand for brings about purpose and drive in an individual. Lack of that independence would mean someone is easily swayable and gullible, limiting his or her attitude and perception towards people in life. Some would argue that the Givers accommodative and adaptive nature makes them likeable and therefore more opportunities would be presented to them, this making them able to climb the corporate ladder faster than others would. They have a strong ability to welcome other people's ideas and thoughts causing people to view them as the go-to guy or girl. Givers solve anything that is put in front of them. And because of their socializing skills they are able to build a network faster than anyone else causing them to be greater at a lot of tasks, especially team based ones.

The giver may be dependent on other people as a source of happiness and success and this might lead him into being exploited for approval and taken advantage of. They can find themselves being naïve, thinking they are winning the trust and approval of others but they may be taken advantage of for the gain of others. This has a lot of hypocrisy in it and because of the constant change of personality to suit the situation, the giver might always struggle being appreciated for whom they truly are. Givers love to "give" and overall have an approachable and calming manner that others love to have around. They just need to be careful when being too nice, because some people out their take it for granted!

Type 3: The Performer

The third personality type is the Performer. He is goal oriented and hugely motivated allowing him or her to achieve great success. Their sole agenda is to make it in life because they are driven by being the odd one out. Most of the time they puts their success before their feelings, opinions and life. To them the best image they can portray of themselves is the revenge they can dish out for being sidelined. They are so obsessed with their image, they don't have time for other things in life which limits their scope and range, lacking to reach people.

They are high achievers mainly because they have dedicated most of their time and life into perfecting their craft. Because they are so focused on achieving their goals, following their dreams and passion, they can lead towards to developing health and psychological issue like fatigue, depression from possible lack of accomplishment. This may be because minimal time is spent taking care of their health and well-being and more on what they need to achieve career wise. The performer and the perfectionist share certain traits, for example, their obsession with achieving goals and doing it in the right way. This meaning that for the performer, nothing less than a hundred percent is accepted and this often leads them being very successful in whatever they do. They can also motivate themselves to overcome hurdles and push others to achieve their dreams and aspirations because they know what it entails. They're very good leaders and this make them exceptional at careers such as sports, acting and taking any entrepreneurial pathway.

The performer should allow life to take place, flow with it and experience all it has to offer. Accept all of its ups and down, and enjoy all experiences that they dive into, so they can draw their own conclusions in anything they tackle in life.

Type 4: The Romantic

The romantic type is about creativity and using art as a medium to channel their views, opinions and feelings. Different people have different ways in which we channel what is inside us. For some other personalities like the perfectionist they prefer keeping it within them and focusing on other things to stop thinking about their situations. The performer channels it to his work and through the high levels of success he attains.

On the other side the romantic has their own way of channeling his feelings, thoughts and attitudes. They do it through art, music, dance and poetry. Sentimental and elaborate when it comes to expressing their thoughts. They are passionate when moving between expressing what other people feel and what they themself feel. The romanticsare emotional individuals who comprehend emotion better than ant other personality group, allowing them to reach other individuals who couldn't reach the comprehension point or understand their emotions through art.

Because of their emotional nature they need time to understand and accept whatever it is they are facing before they can welcome the world into their thoughts. They are very fragile and should be handled with care, because they carry so much emotion.

The romantic can be dynamic when it comes to mood in that he or she may be excited at times or dull depending on what he or she has on their plate at the time. They go through life with an open heart, ready for new experiences and they can take that with them on any task or career they want to tackle.

It's best for Romantics to balance between all emotions that occur and understand that they all happen for a reason. Doing this will draw different reactions for them, teaching them different things that help them develop better interactions and problem-solving skills.

Type 5: The Observer

The fifth personality we are going to look at is the Observer. These people are the introverts in society. They are keen on what takes place around them and do not accept things for what they are. They like to question everything they know and analyze their surroundings to draw meanings and conclusions to everything. The observer tends to dwell alone as he goes about formulating his ideologies. To him, family might be important, but his own interests are of more importance. They don't often indulge in small talk due to their introverted sociological environment and this is because they do not like sharing personal information and tend to keep a lot to themselves. They like to come up with conclusions and solutions from what they have experienced and from the various analyses they have found in their lives.

The observer does not like indulging in small talk and is more comfortable talking or discussing things that they actually excel at or expert in. This is because they fear what they don't know due to the fact that it makes them feel inferior and unknowledgeable. That said though they don't like sharing all the information the have about a particular topic of interest because they're advanced in it. Making it possible that they may be giving too much 'valuable' information away.

The Observers should drop down the walls they have built and share more, accepting more people in their life. This will help them avoid loneliness and also widen their range of knowledge, towards more things that they may be interested in life. Observers are very smart and are considered highly valuable people.

Type 6: The Loyal Skeptic

Two main things characterize this group: their ability to judge characters and situations and their ability to find solutions to problems before they occur. This category of people will always be on the lookout for people and situations that bring them harm and hurt to their families or loved ones. The simple reason being to them that people have different attitudes and intentions and it's up to them to figure them out and come up with quick solutions to whatever they might be. They do not trust easily but when they do, they trust very strongly, making them a great close friend because they will most definitely have your back.

The loyal skeptics are quick to come up with solutions and always remain ahead of the competition or situation, allowing them to be in control of their life making it easier for them to make decisions. They are strategic in how they come up with solutions because they either stop a problem or offer remedies to one empirically. They are courageous and selfless acting to ensure the safety and security of those they care about.

They are very attentive to people and situations because they are strategic. Every detail is relevant in coming up with control or preventive measures to whatever they face. They set high walls that others should prove beyond to protect their own emotional wellbeing from wrong people. They are brave, therefore ask serious questions, leading them to aggressive or pushy attitudes.

The Loyal- Skeptic should welcome more opinions and emotions to their lives and become more accommodating to everyone. This will allow them to grow as individuals, developing a sense of purpose holistically other than their careers just solely. Overall Type 6 is obviously very loyal making them a great friend and person to work with. They are very smart and love to protect those in their life who deserve to be protected.

Type 7: The Epicure

The seventh personality is the epicure, the dynamic crew. These are the ones that value freedom. They are in it for the experience, and they are driven by exploration. Type 7's want to visit different places, learn new things, explore different continents and live in the moment. They are never really stagnant.

This group of personalities are therefore always on the go achieving, realizing and exploring. It gives them so much exposure and make them good people to befriend and talk to because they have a scope of what to talk about and knowledge on the diversified cultures. This is why they should all be appreciated. They are generally very likeable people.

This group though is very uncommitted and undecided on what they want, they hop from one thing to another, and this gives them a sense of purpose and accomplishment, allowing them to draw meaning from their lives. They are all about what works for them and people's opinions don't really faze them. They tend to focus mostly on what they love and go about it whenever and however they see fit. They tend to have an attitude of avoiding their challenges and focus mainly on what's going on correctly. The Epicure group should try to accept that other people hold different opinions and feelings and they do to. Accepting this as a fact and understanding it entirely will help them develop better qualities and become better people all round.

Type 7's like to think as if 'Everything happens for a reason' and this is a powerful mindset to have.

Type 8: The Protector

The protectors often come out and speak on behalf of the rest. They have strong standings and beliefs causing them to be very assertive. They do not back down from a challenge and can be very aggressive and this can be both a good thing and a bad. They air the opinions and thoughts everyone else holds but cannot communicate. They believe that not standing for your rights and defending your opinions leads to exploitation and they term it as weakness.

Protectors are enthusiastic in that they are always on the ready no matter the situation. They await new situations that will come up against what they stand for and defend it fiercely and make sure their opinions are heard and respected by all. Type 8's are powerful people, allowing them to accomplish any task ahead of them. They also put facts as they are, without fear of contradiction.

These individuals, like all the other personalities, have their downfalls, one of them being they are excessive. By this, we mean at times they cross certain lines trying to stand or fight for their rights. It's okay fighting for your rights and enjoying your freedom of expression but all things are done with both sides of the coin flipped. Where one person's rights start is where others end. These people might tend to cross this bridge knowingly or unknowingly from time to time.

The Protector can be quite dominant because their ideals and opinions were not supported. An attitude or perception may have been developed towards themselves if this is the case. Group 8's should try to understand cooperation and mutual understanding, as a means to resolve more issues and make their life easier.

Type 9: The Mediators

The final personalities are the Mediators. Here we have the best of both world's, defenders and challengers dependent on the scenario. The mediators main aim is to bring peace between two torn parties. This means they are welcoming to all opinions and suggestions as they aim to find a balance between all that is presented before them.

They are characterized positively by balance. They find the perfect balance between the two stories and draw sensible or workable conclusions that are accepted by both parties. Secondly, they are accepting, by this I mean that they consider other people's points of view and try to see where they are coming from and why they think as they do. Lastly, they are harmonious, meaning that their main aim is to draw a reasonable and acceptable conclusion to issues and phenomenon in the calmest manner possible.

With positives also comes negative and type 9's have their down sides like all the rest despite their calm and approachable nature. Firstly, they are stubborn because of their drive to get information for resolution provision, they persist an issue until a situation is fully settled and they are also conflict avoidant. They aim to avoid conflict completely, even if at times it might be the best way to find a resolution and this can be cause due to their fear of the situation escalating and going out of hand.

Mediators offer solutions and are open to ideas and opinions which make them standout in a group. The mediators should understand that at times conflict management is essential in drawing conclusions and getting solutions to most issues in society right now.

All these different personalities are what give life its essence. The personality of an individual as seen affects almost everything in life from the way we understand things, relate to people the way we solve situations. Ignorance can make one think that someone is rude or someone else is easy going. Understanding that people handle things differently and taking time to appreciate it and understand it puts a lot of perspective into human life and allows us to tap into human potential. It's important to accept the environment, as it is where everyone is given equal chances to be whom he or she is and express themselves in whatever way. Each personality has its own strengths and weakness and understanding that will allow you to drive further action in life and build greater relationships.

Chapter Three: Personality Type Test

The Riso Hudson Enneagram type indicator will assist you with finding your enneagram type if you're not exactly sure which type resonated with you earlier. This test was initiated by Don Richard Riso and Russ Hudson in 1993 and the research particularly focused on the construction of Rheti, which was the main personality measuring instrument.

Over the course of time, it has been found to be of heuristic value but there is minimal research on a scientific basis, which has been done on the matter. Some of the first steps in the validation of the Riso Hudson enneagram type indicator were made by Warling after collecting information from 153 students that completed the RHETI. More information on the RHETI was done by Dameyer, who showed that retesting and reliability was at a high rate when 82 percent of the people he tested were seen to have the same type they had when they completed the questionnaire a second time.

While a number of enneagram questionnaires have been developed and may show a reasonable amount of reliability, the validity is a bit harder to believe. Utilizing the personality questionnaire as a measure for the enneagram type of an individual can be quite tricky. Part of what makes it so useful when it comes to application is the part where it describes the conscious processes and the motivations that one would not have a lot of access to.

While it is still possible to use the questionnaires the most reliable way is to use the self-assessment questionnaires.

Reliable criterion measures

You should note there are no right answers and no personality type is better than the other. Attempt to answer the questions to the best of your ability in the most honest way possible also. You ought not analyze the questions or think of the exceptions to the rule. You have to be spontaneous and choose the statement which comes closest to the way you have been a lot of your life. If there is difficulty in discovering the personality type because two or more scores are close, then you may find it helpful for you to discuss responses with those who know you very well like a friend, a parent or even a spouse.

There are 38 queries within the sample test. In each case, you need to select the answer which best applies to your scenario. You may skip questions which do not apply though you should not skip questions because they are hard. This test usually takes a duration of about 5 to 10 minutes. For each of the questions they are divided into two options. You need to answer with a designation as A, B, C, D, E, F, G, H, I.

Important:

The table below is the illustration of how the enneagram test works. You are supposed to select one option per question from A to I according to the intensity of agreement. In this way it functions like a Likert scale where A would take the position of the least agreement and I would represent the option for agreeing the most. So in the first question, if you claim to be extremely imaginative and funny then the option taken would be I. Though since my option for this is less agreement, I would go for B. Every question has been answered and marked with a 1 according to the individual's preference for the question. The results are then tabulated as the sum of the answers at the bottom of the graph. In the graph below, the results at the bottom of the chart shows the enneagram type of the individual and they have been illustrated as an example.

From this illustration we can see the top figures are 11, 17 and 13 from options C, D and E.

where we garner the logic of the use of the chart rows of A to I. Each letter from A, B, C, D, E, F, G, H and I represents a personality type as shown in the table below

Columns	A	B	C	D	E	F	G	H	I
Numerical Values									
Personality Type	Nine	Six	Three	One	Four	Two	Eight	Five	Seven

That means that in the example given since D is the most prominent in the results, the enneagram type One is the most prominent for this person doing the test.

So you have a clearer idea, here is an illustration of the test that this person filled in so you have a better idea of how it works:

And don't forget that at the end of this book, there is a clear table where you can work out your own personality type!

		Type	9	6	3	1	4	2	8	5	7	
		Disagree	A	B	C	D	E	F	G	H	I	Agree
1	I have been imaginative and romantic.			1								
	I have been down to earth and pragmatic.				1							
2	I have a tendency to avoid confrontation.						1					
	I have a tendency to go into confrontations.								1			
3	I have usually been direct, idealistic and formal.						1					
	I have usually been diplomatic, ambitious and charming.						1					
4	I have tried to be intense and focused.					1						
	I have a tendency				1							

	Statement																	
	to be fun loving and spontaneous.																	
5	I am a private person and have not tried to mi1 a lot with other people.									1								
	I have been hospitable as an individual and enjoyed welcoming friends to my life.									1								
6	Generally, it has been hard to get a rise so to speak from me.																	1
	Generally, it has been easy to get a rise from me.																1	
7	I have been a high-minded idealist.													1				
	I have been more of a street-smart person or idealist.									1								
8	I have needed to give people affection.													1				
	I have had the preference of maintaining particular distance with individuals.															1		
9	I have needed to													1				

#	Statement													
	give people affection.													
	I have had the preference of maintaining particular distance with individuals.					1								
10	When given a chance at a new e1perience, I have asked myself whether I would enjoy it.				1									
	When presented with new e1periences I have asked mostly whether it would be useful to me.					1								
11	I have had the tendency of focusing too much on my needs.					1								
	I am one of those people that focuses mostly on other people.			1										
12	I come across as being too unsure of things and myself.						1							
	I give off the vibe that I am too sure of myself						1							
13	Other people have depended on the decisiveness and the strength that I give out.							1						
	Other people have depended on the knowledge and insight that I give out.								1					
1	I tend to be more goal									1				

#	Statement													
4	oriented as opposed to being relationship oriented.													
	I tend to be more relationship oriented than goal oriented.												1	
15	I am not very able to speak up for myself.												1	
	I am very outspoken and so I have said what others have wished that they had the nerve to say.											1		
16	It is difficult for me to become more fle1ible and to take things easier.										1			
	It has been hard for me to stop alternatives and to do something which is definite.									1				
17	I have a tendency for procrastination and to be hesitant.							1						
	I have a tendency for being domineering and being courageous.								1					
18	My eagerness to have others depend on me has severally gotten me in trouble with them.									1				
	My hesitation to get involved a lot has gotten me into trouble with other people.									1				
1	Usually, I have had the ability											1		

#	Statement													
9	to put feelings aside and to get the task at hand done.													
	Usually, I have had to work through my emotions before I could get things done.									1				
20	Usually, I am adventurous and have taken risks.									1				
	Usually I am quite meticulous and cautious.											1		
21	I have had tendencies to be serious as a reserved person that likes to discuss things.									1				
	I have tended to be supporting as a giving person that likes the company of other people.								1					
22	I have usually felt the need to perform in the right manner.								1					
	I have often gotten the need to be a pillar of stability.									1				
23	I have been interested usually in the maintenance of stability and peace.										1			
	I have been interested usually in asking tough queries while maintaining some independence.									1				
24	I am very soft							1						

53

#	Statement												
	hearted and sentimental.												
	I am skeptical and hard-nosed in thought processes.			1									
25	I have worried a lot that if I let my guard down that other people are going to take advantage.					1							
	I have worried that I am missing out on connections with other people.						1						
26	My habit of telling others what to do is annoying to my loved ones.					1							
	My habit of being isolated has put others off.						1						
27	Usually when troubles have gotten the best of me, I have treated myself to relieve the stress.							1					
	Usually when troubles have gotten to me, I have been able to work and eventually tune them out.						1						
28	I have not depended on individuals as I have done things solely by myself.				1								
	I have depended on friends and they have known they have the ability to depend on me.					1							

#	Statement							
29	I have had the tendency to be self-absorbed and moody.							1
	I have tendencies to be detached and preoccupied.					1		
30	I like to comfort others when they are distressed and calm them down.				1			
	I like to challenge other people and to shake them up.				1			
31	I have been a serious and earnest or self-disciplined individual.			1				
	I have been a serious a carefree and sociable individual.		1					
32	I have liked to let people know about my strengths or what I can do well.				1			
	I have been very shy about telling others about my strengths and abilities.	1						
33	Having comfort and security is more important to me as compared to pursuing personal interests and preferences.	1						
	Pursuing personal interests has been more significant than having comfort or security.		1					

						A	B	C	D	E	F	G	H	I
3 4	When I have had conflict with other people, I back down on rare occasions.									1					
	When I have had conflict with other individuals, I tended to back down or withdraw.									1					
3 5	I have been known for my sense of humor and unsinkable optimistic attitude.									1					
	I have been known for my quiet strength and e1ceptional amount of generosity as an individual.									1					
3 6	A lot of success has been because of talent in making a good impression								1						
	A lot of success has been attained despite the lack of interest in development of interpersonal skills.								1						
						Total	2	9	1 1	1 7	1 3	9	6	3	2
						Column	A	B	C	D	E	F	G	H	I
						Type	9	6	3	1	4	2	8	5	7

Columns	A	B	C	D	E	F	G	H	I
Numerical Values									
Personality Type	Nine	Six	Three	One	Four	Two	Eight	Five	Seven

In this case, this person is most strongest in Column D so their Personality type would be Type 1: The Reformer.

The following chart shows an example enneagram results for the same test done by another person.

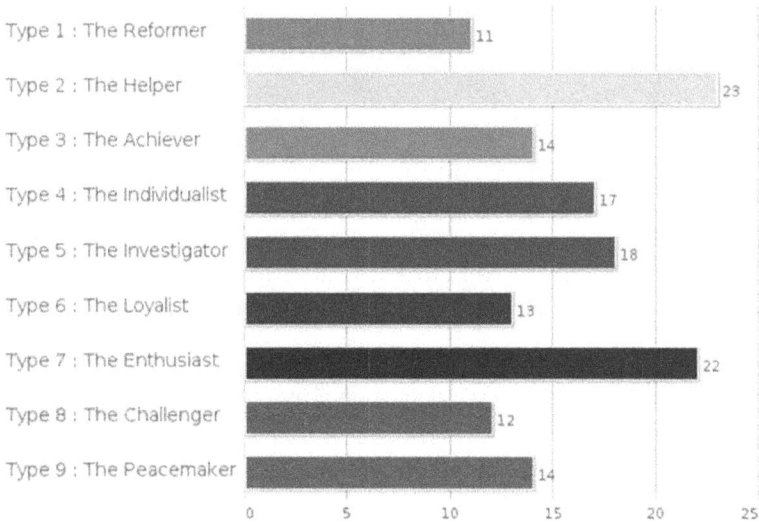

Type	Score
Type 1 : The Reformer	11
Type 2 : The Helper	23
Type 3 : The Achiever	14
Type 4 : The Individualist	17
Type 5 : The Investigator	18
Type 6 : The Loyalist	13
Type 7 : The Enthusiast	22
Type 8 : The Challenger	12
Type 9 : The Peacemaker	14

The discovery of which of the nine types represents one's personality type would be the objective of this test. In the event that you have provided an honest answer for each query which tests a different aspect of your personality, then the accurate type should be displayed as one of the top three scores. If done the right way, the Riso Hudson Enneagram type indicator is going to accurately assess your basic personality type. If the results are not clear, then you need to review your responses as well from an arithmetic point of view. Remember that the questionnaire has 36 questions which are divided into two segments so the total of the answers should be 72.

Remember at the end of this book, there is a clear table where you can work out your personality type!

Chapter Four: Subtypes (27)

Once you have figured out your specific Personality type or maybe you already know what it is. It is now time to have a look at the Subtypes within each Type. These are extra traits within each personality type; you can explore these and take advantage of them for yourself and to better understand the others around you.

There are basic instinctual drives which are necessary for all human experience and they reside in everyone as a primal force. They can be distinguished from personality and often operate from the subconscious yet they are very strong in the direction of how we are as individuals. Though these instincts there are usually, one of the three that may become more dominant. When the main instinct arises with the core enneagram type then a new attribute character is formed.

Take for example if the enneagram was a plate of food then the instinct would determine what you eat first or last. That then relates to the belief of what is good for us or what is thought to be needed in order to get what we want and require in the world. These instincts concern the fundamental intelligences which have come up to make sure people have survived the continuation of the human species. Recent advances in the field of neuroscience have shown the unseen way that these instincts show themselves in the modern world. Now each type of the enneagram personality types has three associated instinctual subtypes that will be mentioned. These are: self-preservation, one on one and the social or sexual element.

The following text will go through how each type is assimilated into the subtypes with consideration for these three elements.

Type 1

Self-preservation : Controlling
The true embodiment of the perfectionist is someone that has a tendency to fuss a lot over everything and wants to make sure that

everything is under control. The subtype key under the self-preservation element in the perfectionist is Worry, which should exacerbate the character itself. The worry element for the type Ones makes them have a strong inner critic which piles on to their self-doubt and strict retentiveness. They become excessively hard on themselves and have a heightened sense of responsibility. They may become very anxious and they do not like to entertain deviances even if it is the smallest detail. Unfortunately, it does not come with an aggressive outlet, which would be advisable as this subtype avoids the expression of anger. They can feel very frustrated when they experience any form of disruption in their activities.

One on one: Stand Out

The subtype key for the perfectionist is they stand out. The reason is their effect on other people. This subtype key allows for an idealistic perspective concerning the way that things need to be causing them to have a sense of entitlement on the way things have to be. It may also make them feel entitled to make others fall into the way they would envision something or someone, putting pressure on others to go according to the way they would like. This subtype key may express anger especially when their efforts to fix the situation are ignored or face resistance.

Social: Non- Adaptable

The subtype key for the perfectionist is being non adaptable. The perfectionist is the one that brings attention to what is right, good and appropriate so they set an example for principled activities. However, this has a flip side as they also have a tendency to be uncompromising even when it comes to the smallest things. High self-discipline and standards are the things that set them apart from the ones that are around them. They are highly motivated by things such as fairness and making things to be in the right way. When they are at their best, they can be systematic thinkers and therefor make very good role models.

Type 2

Self-preservation: Privilege

The subtype key for the giver is referred to as Privilege for the self-preservation element. They are childlike in a way where they can be a bit shy but they can also be charming which makes others want to protect them. The privileged giver is one that wants others to take care of them but does not want to depend fully on others. This making them very protective of their emotions and protective in taking on long term commitments.

One on one: Seduction

The element of one on one inspires the subtype towards seduction, which focuses on the seductive abilities and energies that they attract in intimate relationships. When they are in close relationships with others, they can feel secure and be able to claim what they need in a clear and assertive manner. Though they are gentle, they can be very strong willed and passionate, finding themselves wild at heart. They are also very devoted within these close relationships and they may find it hard to accept boundaries or limits they can go to. As such, it can be a bit hard for them to take no for an answer.

Social: Ambition

The subtype key for the social element in the giver is ambition. The Giver utilizes their strengths in an intelligent way in order to attract and engage communities and broader systems. They may even stand out towards a central or leadership role. They enjoy being with the crowd or up to date with the latest information. The weakness of giving more than they get could be an adapted in a way to distract them from feeling awkward.

Type 3

Self-preservation: Security

The subtype key for the self-preservation element in the achiever is the countertype security. This is a countertype where they do not like advertising strengths and accomplishments in an open manner and they may avoid to be seen as wanting attention. In spite of this matter it is significant for them to be known for their hard work. They have a reliable and efficient subtype and they tend to work towards the right way to do things. They also pursue stability and self-security through their work which may lead to them being workaholics.

One on one: Charisma

The Charismatic subtype of the one on one element for the achiever may focus on their competitiveness towards seeing successful outcomes in other individuals. They usually believe that if the ones around them are to be successful then they should be too. They may also tend to look for affections and the attention of the ones that are closest to them while suppressing their own comfort so that they can host the expectations of others.

Social: Prestige

The social aspect of three has a subtype of prestige as they desire influence and tend to have skills in adjusting to the social requirements of groups and corporations. They are very competitive as they enjoy being the center of attention and confidently market themselves. They work towards being known for their performance and accomplishments. Looking the best and being successful is a very important aspect for the type three social.

Type 4

Self-preservation: Tenacity

The individualist self-preservative is one that is quite resourceful. They suffer stoically and want to be recognized for being able to stomach a lot and not complain. Even if they are very sensitive and might be detached from their feelings, they prefer not to share their issues with other people. This subtype for type 4's have a lot of empathy and they do their best to support people who they believe are experiencing suffering.

One on one: Competition

Individualist's are very intense and can raise their voice to champion their needs and feelings. The subtype of competition for the Type Four can be demanding causing them to escape negative fates by being the best at what they do. They demand that others appreciate the needs they have which can be counter-productive and lead to frustration and anger.

Social: Shame

The social four is very sensitive and connected to the roots of their suffering. There is comfort in the manner that they suffer and they usually attract the admiration from other people. They really want to be understood and this can manifest in self-doubt. This subtype for type 4's can make a comparison to another individual and end up blaming themselves for things that they can or cannot control.

Type 5

Self-Preservation: Castle

The reason why the subtype of the self-preservation type 5 is the castle is because they enjoy their personal space to an extra level. They set out a lot of boundaries and they can live solitary lives with only a few friends. They rather watch social life pass by than participate in it because they enjoy their own company. They are true introverts and prefer not showing a lot of their inner selves, finding it hard to lower their guard without losing a bit of their privacy.

One on one: Confidant

The subtype for the investigator is one that focuses on one or two people in a life that is mostly reserved. They have a strong chemistry with another person and enjoy the connections, however they may live variously through them in some cases. This can lead them to decide to test the loyalty of their partners or resist the potential of them having to be shared with other people.

Social: Totem

The type five social focuses on the big picture and usually looks for the essence and meaning of situations. They tend to connect with experts and groups that have similar high idealism and ones that are detached from the everyday problems or emotions. This subtype for type 5's share values with a lot of enthusiasm, however they still want a big part of their privacy kept to them selves. This may cause them to resist sharing space, or inner resource thus detaching from their environment.

Type 6

Self-preservation: Warmth

In order to feel security, this subtype for type 6's do their best to build alliances and strong relationships with other people. They are very warm in the manner they interact with other people but this is all pointed so that they get what they want in the end. They also repress anger or hesitate to give their honest stand on things as they have a preference to be cautious when at slight risk.

One on One: Intimidation

This subtype for type 6's can come as being quite intimidating and this could lead for one to misdiagnose them as a person. The Six one on one is believed to have a good defense and an even better offense. This approach means they can tackle a lot of situations, especially ones that they initiate and this why other may be a little shy around them.

Social: Duty

This subtype key for the type six is known as Duty. This connects to the usual ideals such as working for a particular cause or even standing up for those who are disadvantaged in society. This subtype key tends to see things in a more polarized manner as compared to the compromising Sixes. They are highly precise and careful and have a preference for following rules and procedure. They also work to encourage compliance to the regulations or the collective norms, making sure that everyone knows the things that are expected of them.

Type 7

Self-Preservation: Network

The energized version of the type seven is someone that knows how to network. They have a family of supporters as they tend to be motivated by wanting what is best for everyone around them. They have a good sense of how to take care of themselves as they like the good things in life. This subtype for type 7's can be very good at rationalizing and defending themselves as well.

One on one: Fascination

The one on one Seven is one that looks at reality through the eyes of the idealist and connects this to every possibility. Their sense of optimism and enthusiasm could be naïve or unrealistic because they want to see the good in everything and everyone. This could make them a possible easy target for people who choose to take advantage of their goodness.

Social: Sacrifice

This is the countertype that works against self-interest for the type Seven. They are very generous and could be confused as a giver as they have strong ideals to be of service in order to create a world which is better. They are willing to sacrifice their needs in order to satisfy those of a larger group that they support. In the end, they can be a bit judgmental concerning selfishness when it comes to them or other individuals. The social subtype for type 7's, highly value being appreciated for the sacrifices that they make for the good of the group.

Type 8

Self-Preservation: Satisfaction

The type 8 self-preservation subtype is one that is productive and seems to be very effective. They seem to be confident even in situations, which are challenging. They play the role of the guardian angel for a lot of people as they seem like a pillar of fortitude. However when their needs are not being met they can become resentful and intolerant. Making a no-nonsense approach so that they get what they want without having to apologize or feel any guilt.

One on one: Possession

This subtype represents the most rebellious archetype of the type Eight which is quite provocative, breaking the rules as they please. They are very impulsive and have a desire to be intense making them willing to disrupt and provoke others if to accumulate influence and power. They also have the desire to serve a cause, which is worthy as long as it's from a point where they are leaders.

Social: Solidarity

The social type Eight is one that utilizes their influence in serving other people and drive for the support of other people. They can be very sensitive to injustice and social norms, which are not fair to everyone as they are loyal and protective, especially towards their close friends. Even though they have a preference of not being very vulnerable they also invite good feedback from people that are close to them.

Type 9

Self-preservation: Appetite

This subtype for personality type 9 self-preservation is known as appetite. This is concerned with the needs of the body center with such activities like eating or sleeping for their wellbeing and comfort. They like to use activities, which are a strategy towards comfort for themselves through the fulfillment of their appetites. Peace and time alone are some of the significant things that they need because they value their privacy. They can be irritable especially when other people come into their area and upset the balance of things.

One on one: Fusion

The subtype key for the one on one Nine fuses strongly with others in relationships so that they can feed their sense of comfort and themselves. They are much more secure when they are in romantic relationships or when they are partnered with others because they find it hard to do things by themselves. They are not likely to pay attention to their desires and passions as they get caught up in going along with the preferences of other people, even if it would mean the sacrifice of their needs.

Social: Participation

The social subtype key for the nine participates and regularly becomes the mediator or the one that facilitates in groups. They place their issues aside and maintain a happy look in order to avoid having to burden other people. They make sacrifices in order to meet the needs of the group because they gain a lot of comfort from being part of things in bigger groups. They work hard to keep those in their life happy, however they may encounter potential risk of becoming a workaholic, hiding their pain in their stresses.

Chapter Five: Self-Awareness And Growth Through Your Personality Type

Now that you have discovered your personality type, it is important that you consider actions and steps that will allow you the joys of personal growth to become more self-aware. As you would guess, different personalities have different actions and recommendations for the journey of self-awareness. Therefore, let us examine each of these individually in order to help you identify what works best for your type.

1. Type One: The Reformer

The main concern for you is to reclaim your serenity and learn to be Zen. In order for you to grow as a person, you must learn to release your resistance and accept that just because things do not seem to be perfect it does not mean that they are bad or unworthy. In order to achieve this, it is advisable that you relax; taking time for yourself and release the mental burden that you need to do everything. It might be difficult to start but you need to understand that what you do not accomplish or do, will not always result in a disaster of chaos. Even though it feels like you are the savior of the world, it is not the case and therefore you should not push to be Superman.

As a type One, you should learn to embrace not only your imperfections but those of others as well. This will help you when resolving conflicts with others as you will become more open minded to the opinions of others. Doing this will allow you to be more forgiving of mistakes, which can help you as a giver of knowledge. Speaking of knowledge, because you have a natural talent of teaching others, it is important to learn to be patient especially when it comes to change. You may embrace change quickly but for the ones you teach, it might not come as easy. However, it does not mean that it will never happen.

Use positive affirmations to guide you such as 'Life is perfect as it is', 'I choose to be flexible, adaptable and embrace change', and 'I choose to be kind, compassionate and understanding'. This will help you get in touch with your emotions while still maintaining the intelligent, reasonable, and logical side that is in you.

2. Type Two: The Helper

If you are a helper seeking personal growth, your area of concern should be to reclaim humility through becoming more conscious of your own motives. To start, you should learn to differentiate between meeting your needs and not being too needy; it will stop you from being clingy and turn you into an emotionally aware person.

Because you give love unconditionally, you do well in relationships. However, it may often draw you away from taking care of your own needs because you are too concerned with fulfilling your partner's needs. Keep your genuine loving nature but also put in more effort into caring for yourself and meeting your needs first.

As it has already been established, you enjoy helping others and it is a spirited nature that you should continue to do. You can adjust it slightly in two main ways; first, ask people what they really need before doing something for them or helping them. Second, fight the temptation of reminding people what you have done for them after you have done it. Instead, let it be and leave it to them to either thank you or not, rather than reminding them and making them feel uneasy. Your positive affirmations should range between loving others and yourself unconditionally and being perfectly clear about your intentions.

3. Type Three: The Achiever

An achiever's true growth and self-development comes in the form of being truthful. This starts with being honest with yourself and others, especially about your feelings. Be authentic by resisting the temptation to brag or impress others. Take some time off from your busy day to connect with another person you care about; it will allow you to become more loving and caring in your relationships.

Your ambition is a great quality that you should hold on to; you can improve this by allowing yourself regular breaks to not exhaust yourself. These breaks give you the opportunity to get in touch with yourself and recharge your batteries. Taking a break will also help you understand that success does not rest on your shoulders alone; allowing you to consider making a team.

Develop yourself through avoiding doing what is acceptable just to be accepted; take time to discover your values instead. The most important positive affirmation you should repeat to yourself is that you are authentic despite your mistakes and imperfections.

4. Type Four: The Individualist

The most important thing for you is to understand that your feelings are not a true source of support. That being said, try avoid working according to your mood; meaningful work should not wait until you are in the right mood. No matter how small the contribution may be, making contributions through work will help you discover your talents and special skills.

In order to develop your self-confidence, you should bury the feeling of 'not being together' and put yourself in the path of good. The best way to do this is to take on a challenge whether it be physically or emotionally; at work or in a relationship- the commitment will bring out the best in you. If the challenge gets you stressed, you should give yourself time and space to de-stress through communicating with your loved ones.

As much as you may enjoy lengthy conversations in your imagination, you should take it down a notch and instead use this time to build relationships with your loved ones through actual conversations. Practice equanimity and find joy in the present.

5. Type Five: The Investigator

For type five, you receive spiritual growth and self-awareness when you give yourself to others. It is normal to have conflicts and you should allow yourself to work things out; it will make you work well when it comes to resolving conflicts. Having even one friend whom you are comfortable conflicting with is a real bonus to your personal growth.

Because you are so intense, it may be difficult to unwind and let go; this can easily lead to unhealthy ways of coping with stress such as drug abuse and alcohol. When you get stressed, turn to exercise or biofeedback techniques; it will turn your nervous energy into helpful motivation to keep at it.

Your mental capacity is indeed an extraordinary gift but it can take you out of the here and now. Possibly drowning you in your mental capacity. Try as much as possible to stay with your physicality by speaking out your thoughts and ideas with others around you. This will not only make you a better communicator but it will also help you get your needs met.

6. Type Six: The Loyalist

Your spiritual path as a type six is to let go of fear because after all, you attract what you think. Learn to be present in your own anxiety because after all, people are more anxious than you think and it is not unusual. If you get in touch with your anxiety and pick up on it, you will be able to manage it and may even be able to turn it into a powerful tonic that energizes you and makes you more productive.

When under stress, you may find yourself to be testy, angry, or simply competitive. This can make you blame others for your own shortcomings; therefore, become aware of your pessimism and find creative ways of dealing with it. Learn to point out what makes you overreact and learn to manage your thoughts about these topics. You should always remind yourself that things are not as bad as they seem and that the 'bad' is mostly your imagination overreacting. Managing this helps you solve problems faster and in a more logical way.

Trust is a big issue for this type of personality but in order for you to grow; you need to become more trusting. Look for people in your life who care about you and have themselves offered to put their trust in you. Open up to them about your emotions, thoughts, and needs, allowing yourself to get close to them. Because you have a natural gift for getting people to like you, tell them how you feel about them and you will notice that you become less anxious and more grounded and comfortable in your own skin.

7.   Type Seven: The Enthusiast

Growth for the enthusiast is achieved when you are no longer dependent on the highs of life because you will be able to pace yourself and immerse yourself into the real nature of existence which does include some lows. One way to do this is by observing your impulses and not giving into them; the more you resist, the more you will be able to focus on what is truly important.

When it comes to experiences, it is better to choose quality over quantity. Do not let yourself miss what is happening now because you were too busy anticipating the future. The present has a lot to teach you, unlike the future and as much as you wish, you will never be able to predict or completely prepare for anything.

Because you are a visionary, you should take opportunities that will allow you to think and generate new ideas. You will realize with time that doing this gives you joy, brings out social versions of yourself and you will actually discover a few talents.

8.   Type Eight: The Challenger

As a type eight, you realize that you overvalue power and love to be in control of everything. However, if you are to grow, you need to come to the conclusion that true strength is in forgiveness because it is a stronger sign of courage. When in power, ensure that you act as a leader and not a boss; lead by example rather than just giving out orders. You will become a better communicator and worker for that matter.

As much as you think the world is against you, you should come to terms with the fact that they look up to you to set a bar. Believing that these people are against you, hurts your relationships because you end up alienating yourself from them. Identify the people who are on your side and let them know that you also care for them; this will not only improve your relationships but it will also give you a lot more self-confidence.

Positive affirmations that should govern your life include 'I can be gentle and strong at the same time', 'I extend a helping hand to those who need support', and 'I embrace every part of me, including my weaknesses'.

9. Type Nine: The Peacemaker

Though you may be used to daydreaming, growth means you remain in tune with people. Attempt to be more involved both mentally and physically so you can be an active member of society. It will improve your interpersonal skills and turn your relationships into opportunities for better communication.

In order to become more aware of your body and emotions, you should engage yourself in exercises. Not only is it a healthy way of forming self-discipline but it is also helping you increase your awareness of your feelings and emotions. Body-awareness will help you to concentrate and direct your attention in other parts of your life. It is also a great way to release stress and aggressions.

Hold positive affirmations such as being in touch with the world around you and working on your personal needs close to your heart. These will give you a surprisingly calm energy and help you understand that you do not need to lose yourself to others in order for you to be accepted, loved, or to simply keep the harmony.

Chapter Six: Enneagram and Relationships/Friendships

Relationships occupy a significant part of our time and attention and so they remain as one of the big mysteries in life. The enneagram can provide the archetype personalities for different individuals and suggests the pairings that are adequate with the potential advantages and issues that can come about with each pairing.

Enneagram Ones and Twos

The Ones and Twos are quite complementary as both provide each other an example of their qualities due to their attraction towards servicing roles and occupations. Their relationship is built on shared values, as they like to be on a path together. The enneagram Twos bring nurturing while the Ones do not easily allow themselves to relax. The Ones bring conscientiousness, consistency and integrity so they would not feel as though they have been abandoned. Now the trouble is that Twos may see the Ones as being unconcerned with others and not empathetic. They may feel like the Ones have idealistic ideals but do not have a lot of compassion for the real people.

The Two type enneagram can also pair with the Four which may result is a warm and passionate couple when both parties share their feelings in an open manner. They can be very good for each other as the Twos bring social skills and energy, which allows the Four to have confidence to interact very easily with other people. Type Fours brings a lot of creativity and have a good sense of humor. They also bring subtlety and emotional depth into the relationship through a sense of sensuality. On the flip side, the enneagram of Twos and Fours make better colleagues and friends than life partners. They both have a lot of needs which makes them cling to those who would respond to them adequately. Over the long term there can be competition for attention from one sector. At the same time, the Twos can find the fours to be very moody and led by their impulses too much. They may also see a

Four as being too hyper absorbed and hyper sensitive. On the other hand, the Four might see the Two as being too emotionally needy and desperate for other people to like them or seek them. They may be secretly envious though of the social abilities of the Two and the positive reactions they get from others though to the point they feel socially inept as they become intimidated. Being careful of these encounters and realizing them will bond a stronger connection.

Enneagram Type Three and Three

The type Three is a good pair with another Three as they bring an equal amount of effort to the table. They are both hard workers and always look for a way to improve their situation. They can therefore be very effective as a team, making them likely to be very successful in their endeavors. They are also very respectful of each other's privacy and would likely avoid drama within the relationship as they give space to each other to pursue their interests. The trouble with this union is one or both of the Threes might start feeling the relationship is taking time from their career and the pursuit towards success. One might feel that they are sacrificing their careers and potential for the sake of keeping the relationship together even though the other may be gaining mileage. This usually happens when the couple gets children and one spouse has to sacrifice their career to help out at home or when one travels and the other follows them in order to sacrifice.

Enneagram Type Four Goes with Type Five

Both the Fours and Fives bring particular richness and qualities to their development. The Fours may bring some artistry and emotional temperament as well as introspection and sensitivity in themselves. They are both private types and like depth as they do not mind taking the time to explore things to the full extent. The Fives bring an intellectual temperament as well as the habit of asking questions. Both of the types also bring a good sense of humor and love of the outlandish which can make the relationship appear to be quirky and unique. The Fours help the Fives to remain in contact with themselves and their feelings as they have mutual tolerance for things that may come up and neither is shocked.

The trouble that comes with the pairing of the Four with the Five is the Four is an emotional type causing them to want more contact, which may result in too much demand. The Fives are thinking sorts and they may try for more space and detachment within the relationship which means they can become more private. The Fours may feel that the Fives are too intellectual or feel that the Fives are being too analytical towards the relationship rather than just being sympathetic with their emotional requirements and their situation. They might also have the feeling that the Fives are unavailable or uncaring to what they need. The Fives on the other hand look at it as the Four is a bottomless pit of needs that drain their time and energy. The Fives may also feel that the emotionality shows a lack of rationality or is a sign of immaturity. Speaking and opening up to one another is highly important for this pair.

Enneagram Type Ones and Sixes

Another pairing that would make a good team is the Ones and the Sixes and a lot of the time they are misidentified with each other. Both of the types can be very hard workers and have a strong sense of integrity and duty. Both of them care about the truth and being committed as they both want to serve other people and improve their world. Obviously they have the ability to bring other qualities which are their own. The Ones can bring a lot of mental clearness and rationality as they think very well when they are under pressure. They are also sure of themselves as compared to the Sixes. The Sixes on the other hand allow for warmth, better emotional response and generosity which can be endearing, making the Ones think again about their positions. The Sixes may have the chance to connect with people in a direct way as compared to the way the Ones tend to do. These qualities are quite attractive and they can make the couple a bit dynamic and yet a stable team. That is because they feel they can count on each other.

The trouble with this pairing is seen in the points of crises. As the level of stress continues to rise, the Ones can become judgmental of their partner and themselves. They may have the attitude of having all work and no play which seems they are a bit joyless and even difficult to be around. This enables resentment and accusations, allowing for a lot of bickering which can wear on the Sixes more than it would on a fellow One. If the tensions continue, then a Six would become more evasive and defensive as they will also want to stay away from their partner because they do not want conflict. To their misfortune, the Six is going to find it hard to talk in a direct manner concerning their fears and so there is not a lot which becomes aired out.

Enneagram Type Six and Three

This is not a common pairing but surprisingly these types can work as a team. The Threes bring a lot of energy and hard work to communicate and connect with individuals. This allows for unlimited potential for the relationship and for the personal growth of an individual. The Sixes can also bring compassion and a lot of quality comfort for the Threes that are experiencing stress. The Three may also pick up on the compassionate nature of the Sixes and then learn to open their hearts in a deeper way to those who are not as privileged.

Both of them have strong feelings of supporting each other towards goals, whether it is in finances or developing their talents. They both foster mutual levels of respect for the different traits each bring and the interests that they may invest within. The Three is also good for the Six's confidence building up their self-esteem. The Sixes may offer to support the Threes as well without them feeling smothered and this is important. Sixes may also assist the Threes to be a part of something which is greater than themselves like a church or a political organization and so they help them to see the big picture. On the flip side, they may also be able to bring out the worst attributes in each other if the relationship is not healthy. They are both competitive and can be workaholics as they both look externally for being reassured to make up for their secret insecurities. Both want to be socially accepted for the things they do and they like to avoid looking at their feelings or discussing their emotions. At the worst, both can be evasive and dishonest concerning their actions and the way they feel. They can deteriorate the partnership to the level it is at robotic functioning.

Enneagram Type Six and Eight

The type Sixes like to feel safe while the type Eights want to be the protective one and this is why they're a god pairing. One wants loyalty while the other gives it freely as their quality. The type Eight is also very focused and has a very intentional manner of being active and during this the Type Six can keep busy and try to not show how anxious they are. The type Eights are very impulsive before fully thinking things through and then weighing the consequences. The type Sixes on the other hand can be helpful to the Eights through looking at the worst case scenarios and the potential disadvantages and creation of backups. The type Sixes are skilled at the preparation for eventualities which may come up. Type Eights are direct about the people that they are and where they stand and this usually builds trust with the type Sixes. The Type Eights may learn to pay attention to the downside of their plans and try to manage them. The Type Sixes can excel in areas of research and bring some intellectual stimulation to the union between them and the Eights.

Enneagram Type Seven and Nine

These are one of the most often viewed pairings of the types as they bring a good mix of qualities. At the basic level, they are both positive perspective types that are upbeat about things and like to avoid anything negative in their lives. They are also both friendly and sociable, making them good with forgiveness and able to compromise to the best of their ability. On a social side, sevens are more active as compared to the nines and so they make the plans and have multiple interests. The sevens are also mentally fast and self-confident as they may be open to new experiences. The nines though bring support, steadiness and acceptance for the pairing. They are also more sympathetic and soft hearted as compared to the sevens. The trouble though is neither the nines nor the sevens are adept when it comes to working through painful elements in their relationship. Both of them prefer that things remain on the positive side. They tend to be both edgy and anxious when they are under stress and so they might take this out on each other rather than work things out as a couple. Between the two of them, the sevens are much more equipped to talk about what is bothering them as compared to the nines.

Bottom line

In order to individuate according to Carl Jung, there are some things that we can get for ourselves such as discipline, focus, containment and loyalty. These are all attributes that are attractive in getting a partner, however not every enneagram type has equal portions of the above. The main thing to note is you do not have to go for the enneagram matches that are advised in the text as you can build your traits to what you would like to be or what you think your essence is. You have to remember that your reactions are all about you one hundred percent of the time. Your partner is a good mirror for you to see yourself clearly because they are the representation of how you treat those closest to you.

Analyzing each personality type and the most compatible types will help you grow quicker and stronger. It is important to also remember that reading about the types isn't just for relationship purposes. This can immensely help you towards figuring out who you are and the best way you can live a more calming and fulfilled life, taking advantage of the traits in which you excel at.

Conclusion

Congratulations on finishing Enneagram. Hopefully you now have a better understanding of your personality type and those of others you know. Enneagram is a powerful guide towards finding your strengths and using them to your advantage as well as finding the strengths of others around you such as friends and family so you can use that to build your relationships with one another.

If you found this book helpful in anyway please leave a positive review on Amazon as it allows me to keep producing quality books. Thanks.

low is a clear Table where you can do the Enneagram test to find your Personality Type!

										Typ e	9	6	3	1	4	2	8	5	7
										Disa gree	A	B	C	D	E	F	G	H	I	A g r e e
1	I have been imaginativ e and romantic.																		
	I have been down to earth and pragmatic.																		
2	I have a tendency to																		

	avoid confrontation.															
	I have a tendency to go into confrontations.															
3	I have usually been direct, idealistic and formal.															
	I have usually been diplomatic, ambitious and charming.															
4	I have tried to be intense and focused.															
	I have a tendency to be fun loving and spontaneous.															
5	I am a private person and have not tried to mi1 a lot with other people.															
	I have been hospitable as an individual and enjoyed welcoming friends to my life.															
6	Generally, it has been hard to get a rise so to speak from me.															
	Generally, it has been easy															

	to get a rise from me.																					
7	I have been a high-minded idealist.																					
	I have been more of a street-smart person or idealist.																					
8	I have needed to give people affection.																					
	I have had the preference of maintaining particular distance with individuals.																					
9	I have needed to give people affection.																					
	I have had the preference of maintaining particular distance with individuals.																					
10	When given a chance at a new e1perience, I have asked myself whether I would enjoy it.																					
	When presented with new e1periences I have asked mostly whether it would be useful to me.																					
11	I have had the tendency of focusing too much on my needs.																					
	I am one of those																					

	people that focuses mostly on other people.																
12	I come across as being too unsure of things and myself.																
	I give off the vibe that I am too sure of myself																
13	Other people have depended on the decisiveness and the strength that I give out.																
	Other people have depended on the knowledge and insight that I give out.																
14	I tend to be more goal oriented as opposed to being relationship oriented.																
	I tend to be more relationship oriented than goal oriented.																
15	I am not very able to speak up for myself.																
	I am very outspoken and so I have said what others have wished that they had the nerve to say.																
16	It is difficult for me to become more flexible and to take things easier.																
	It has been hard for me to																

	stop alternatives and to do something which is definite.																
17	I have a tendency for procrastination and to be hesitant.																
	I have a tendency for being domineering and being courageous.																
18	My eagerness to have others depend on me has severally gotten me in trouble with them.																
	My hesitation to get involved a lot has gotten me into trouble with other people.																
19	Usually, I have had the ability to put feelings aside and to get the task at hand done.																
	Usually, I have had to work through my emotions before I could get things done.																
20	Usually, I am adventurous and have taken risks.																
	Usually I am quite meticulous and cautious.																
21	I have had tendencies to be serious as a reserved person that likes to discuss things.																
	I have tended to be supporting																

	as a giving person that likes the company of other people.																			
2 2	I have usually felt the need to perform in the right manner.																			
	I have often gotten the need to be a pillar of stability.																			
2 3	I have been interested usually in the maintenance of stability and peace.																			
	I have been interested usually in asking tough queries while maintaining some independence.																			
2 4	I am very soft hearted and sentimental.																			
	I am skeptical and hard-nosed in thought processes.																			
2 5	I have worried a lot that if I let my guard down that other people are going to take advantage.																			
	I have worried that I am missing out on connections with other people.																			
2 6	My habit of telling others what to do is annoying to my loved ones.																			

	My habit of being isolated has put others off.																		
2 7	Usually when troubles have gotten the best of me, I have treated myself to relieve the stress.																		
	Usually when troubles have gotten to me, I have been able to work and eventually tune them out.																		
2 8	I have not depended on individuals as I have done things solely by myself.																		
	I have depended on friends and they have known they have the ability to depend on me.																		
2 9	I have had the tendency to be self-absorbed and moody.																		
	I have tendencies to be detached and preoccupied.																		
3 0	I like to comfort others when they are distressed and calm them down.																		
	I like to challenge other people and to shake them up.																		
3 1	I have been a serious and earnest or self-disciplined individual.																		
	I have been a																		

	serious a carefree and sociable individual.																			
3 2	I have liked to let people know about my strengths or what I can do well.																			
	I have been very shy about telling others about my strengths and abilities.																			
3 3	Having comfort and security is more important to me as compared to pursuing personal interests and preferences.																			
	Pursuing personal interests has been more significant than having comfort or security.																			
3 4	When I have had conflict with other people, I back down on rare occasions.																			
	When I have had conflict with other individuals, I tended to back down or withdraw.																			
3 5	I have been known for my sense of humor and unsinkable optimistic attitude.																			
	I have been known for my quiet strength and e1ceptional amount of generosity as an individual.																			
3 6	A lot of success has been because of talent in making a good impression																			
	A lot of success has been attained despite the lack of																			

interest in development of interpersonal skills.																			
										Total									
										Colum n	A	B	C	D	E	F	G	H	I
										Type	9	6	3	1	4	2	8	5	7

Whatever column has the highest number represents what personality type you are!

www.ingramcontent.com/pod-product-compliance
Lightning Source LLC
Chambersburg PA
CBHW072153020426
42334CB00018B/1988